Also Availabl

GET RID OF YOUR HEAD TRASH ABOUT MONEY

How to Avoid the 3 Massive Money Mistakes
Even Smart People Make

by Noah St. John

#1 Bestselling author of *The Book of AFFORMATIONS®*
Founder of The Afformations® Solution and Power Habits® Academy

Praise for Noah St. John

"Noah's method is one of the most significant breakthroughs in the study of success in decades. If you want to eliminate the fear of success and live the life you've imagined, you owe it to yourself to get his programs."

— Jack Canfield
Chicken Soup for the Soul

"Using humor and down-to-earth language, Noah gives you a step-by-step method to live the life you want and deserve."

— John Gray, Ph.D.
Men Are from Mars, Women Are from Venus

"Noah St. John speaks the language we all want to understand: how to make the most of your life and career."

— Harvey Mackay
Swim with the Sharks Without Being Eaten Alive

"Noah St. John's work is about discovering within ourselves what we should have known all along—we are truly powerful beings with unlimited potential."

— Stephen Covey
The 7 Habits of Highly Effective People

"You'll never get your foot off the brake and find the success you dream of until you take Noah's advice to heart!"

— T. Harv Eker
Secrets of the Millionaire Mind

"Noah is a brilliant guy who brings tremendous insight into this problem of embracing success he quite accurately observes in people."

— Neale Donald Walsch
Conversations with God

"Noah has created something magical. I've been studying personal growth for more than 25 years and his insights take it to the next level!"

— Jenny McCarthy
Host of The Jenny McCarthy Show

"If you are looking for a spark to light your inner flame, Noah's methods will IGNITE your passion within."

— John Lee Dumas
Entrepreneur on Fire

"Noah St. John has created a masterpiece. I truly enjoyed this book and believe that I am already on a better path toward success as I implement the principles Noah has so eloquently shared."

— Nathan Osmond
Nashville Recording Artist

"Noah's work is awesome and sooooo very needed in this world right now!"

— Marie Forleo
Host of MarieTV

"Noah's methods can literally transform your life—and help you create the masterpiece you truly want and are capable of achieving."

— John Assaraf
author of The Answer

"I went from $60,000 in debt to a six-figure income in six months because of Noah's trainings."

— Susan Sherayko
Television Producer

"I'd spent over $30,000 on self-improvement products with few results. By following Noah's program, my sales tripled in one month – and by the end of the year, my sales increased 560% and I was named New Agent of the Year."

— Brandon Handy
Allegis Financial Partners

"I made my annual income in just 44 days following Noah's program."

— Ray Higdon
Network Marketing Leader

"I went from $5,000 to $75,000 in monthly sales as a result of following Noah's Power Habits® Formula. Best of all, I'm working FEWER hours than before, even with this increase in income. Thank you Noah for taking the lid off my thinking and letting me know I could have the BEST!"

— Sheila Valles
Direct Sales Professional

Contents

Who This Book Is For

This book is for people who desire to make more money, help more people, and have more fun!

It's for people who want to get rid of their head trash around money.

It's for men and women who want more FREEDOM – more time freedom, financial freedom, emotional freedom, and location freedom.

Does this sound like you?

If so, you're in the right place!

Listen, I know you have a lot of things going on – a million-and-one distractions pulling at you, however...

This book is all about YOU.

Your money, your life, your legacy. I'll be talking about all of these things in the pages that follow.

That's one reason I encourage you to give yourself the gift of allowing yourself to focus and fully enjoy the pages you're about to read.

I'm also going to pull back the curtain on my own personal (and mostly embarrassing) story...

And share real-life case studies of my coaching clients and Mastermind students who have used my Formula to get amazing results.

Yes, this method is PROVEN – which means that it's been tried and tested by people in every business, market, and niche you can think of (yes, even yours!).

So whether you've been a student of mine for years, or this is the first time you've heard of me, I will reveal things in this book that I've never publicly revealed before.

That's one reason I'm excited that you're reading this book today...

Because when you follow my Formula and start taking these simple, proven steps...

Your stress level will go down...

Your bank account will go up...

And life will start to get fun again!

So let's get started...

Surviving Zip Lining: A True Story

Have you ever tried zip lining? If you haven't, have you ever wanted to try it?

Zip lining is an adventure sport where you strap yourself into a harness and go zooming through the air suspended on a steel cable.

After that description, maybe you're thinking, "I would NEVER try zip lining!"

Well, the truth is that I'm a total nerd. Now my wife is an adventure junkie – so of course we match perfectly...

Before we got married, my bride-to-be and I were planning our honeymoon, and she says to me, "Let's go zip lining!"

And I'm thinking, "How can I get out of this?"

But of course I didn't want to look like a wimp to my bride-to-be, so I – with a great deal of hesitation – agreed.

On our honeymoon, I find myself on the Caribbean island of St. Kitts, a stunningly beautiful gem of an island. However, because I'm so nervous about our upcoming zip lining adventure, I can't relax and enjoy the scenery...

We arrive at the zip lining location. We have 3 large, muscular men as our guides. They take us through a training process and give us harnesses and other gear.

Then they put our zip lining group in a truck and drive us up a windy dirt road on the side of a mountain in the middle of a Caribbean rainforest. My heart is pounding a mile a minute. We go up, up, and up for what seems like forever...

Then we pile out of the truck and climb up a set of wooden stairs to a small platform high up on the mountaintop.

One of the big guides straps on his gear, hooks onto the zip line, turns to us and says, "See you on the other side!" and suddenly...

Zzzzzzzzzzzzzzzzip! Off he goes off into infinity.

Gulp, says I.

Then one of the other guides, who is standing there on the platform with the rest of us tourists, turns to me and says, "Okay, you're next."

Me??, I'm thinking. *Why do I have to go next?*

Yet again, I don't want to look scared in front of my new bride (even though I'm terrified), so I walk over to the edge of the platform and look down...

And my brain says to me: *"We are definitely going to die."*

In my fear-filled state at that moment, I realize that in the next few seconds, I have three options that will define the rest of my life...

Option 1: Back down because I'm too scared.

My first thought is to go back to where we came from, go back to the safety of the truck, go back to my old life because I don't want to die.

But then I realize that that's not really an option...

Because the truck has already gone.

Which means I would have to walk at least two miles down a windy dirt road on the side of a mountain in the middle of a Caribbean rainforest… which means I could get eaten by crocagators or whatever is lurking in the jungle on this island.

So I realize that that option doesn't actually exist.

Option 2: Stay right where I am. Don't move. Don't go forward.

My second thought is that I could stay right where I am, don't move and don't go forward.

But then I realize that that's not an option either…

Because how will I get down from this platform at the top of a mountain? It's not like they're going to just leave me standing there like an idiot (even though that's what I'd look like if I chose this option).

And how will I face my new bride after wimping out like that?

So that's not really an option either.

Finally, I review my other, and only realistic, option…

Option 3: Face my fears and step forward.

As I'm standing there at the top of a mountain in the Caribbean rainforest pondering my certain demise, suddenly a thought occurs to me…

"Hey, wait a minute…That guide who went before me… He's bigger than me…Which means he weighs more than I do…And he didn't die. So maybe I won't die!"

Then I remember that they took us through this training process and I remember seeing pictures of everyone from little kids to grandparents doing zip lining, and I'm like...

"Are you really going to wimp out when people just like you weren't afraid to do this??"

So I take a deep breath, and with my mind still screaming *"We're going to die!"* at me, take that one step into infinity, and...

Wheeeeeeeeeeeeeeee!

It's so fun, so exhilarating, I can't wait to do it again!

Noah & Babette after Noah faced his fear and took that step of faith

In fact, here's a picture of me and my wife after I stepped forward in the face of fear in that Caribbean rainforest...

In fact, I had such a great time that today, I lead zip lining adventures with my DREAM Mastermind!

Yes, I have a mastermind program called The DREAM Mastermind, where I work with entrepreneurs and small business owners to help them build their business to new heights over the course of one to three years. We sometimes go on fun adventures so they can prove to themselves that they, too, can overcome their fears like I did.

Here's a picture of one of our DREAM Mastermind adventures in Orlando, Florida...

Noah with his DREAM Mastermind clients

The Moral of The Story

Our brains often tell us things that simply aren't true.
You see, your brain's main job is to keep you SAFE –
to make sure you don't die. But have you ever noticed
that sometimes "playing it safe" is the most dangerous
thing you can do?

Because not only will you miss out on life, you won't
allow yourself to grow and experience the best that life
has to offer.

So the next time you're "on the platform" faced with a
seemingly life-or-death choice like I had on that zip line
platform at the top of a mountain in the Caribbean
rainforest, realize that you, too, have those same 3
choices...

Option 1: Try to go back to the way things were.
(Sadly, this isn't possible.)

Option 2: Stay right where you are. (This isn't
possible, either.)

Option 3: (The only choice we actually have) Face your
fears and step forward.

You see, one of the funny things about life is that it
doesn't allow us to go back or stay in place – as much as
we would like to.

It's true: As much as we want to go back to the way
things were in the "good old days" (which often weren't
that good to begin with)...

Or stay right where we are (because we're afraid to move forward)...

Those choices don't really exist.

They are false options, because they simply aren't possible.

That's why the only actual choice is to step forward.

Here's The Great News

However, the great news is that once you make that decision and take that first step – even though it might feel scary, even terrifying – I'll bet you'll find that the doing of the thing isn't half as bad as the thinking about doing it.

Have you ever noticed that to be true in your own life?

You're thinking about the thing, getting more and more worried, more scared, more stressed...

Then one day, you finally decide to "JUST DO IT" and...

Find out it wasn't so bad, after all.

You've done this too, haven't you?

Oh, and one more thing...

The next time you're thinking of trying something new, ask yourself this simple question...

"Am I the first person to attempt this, or have other people done it before me and lived to talk about it?"

The truth is, if we're thinking about doing something new (for us), most of us like to know that other people other people have done it before us – that we're not the first person to do it.

Want proof? Have you ever read a review of a restaurant or hotel you're considering going to? Have you ever read a review of a book or movie you're thinking about buying, or even renting? Have you ever read reviews on Amazon, TripAdvisor, or Yelp before you purchased something on those sites?

Why do we do this? Because we want the comfort of knowing that someone else has done and liked the thing we're thinking about doing or buying. If other people like or have benefited from something, then we're far more likely to "take the plunge" for ourselves.

That's one reason this book includes real-life case studies from a few of my clients and students, because I hope that seeing their success stories will encourage you to know that you can do it, too.

Bottom line: Sometimes it just takes one step to change your life.

And if you take that step with me, I promise that I'll catch you.

Now let me tell you a story about the worst day of my life...

The Worst Day of My Life

In just a moment, I'm going to give you my 5 proven steps to get rid of your head trash around money. Yet first I'd like to share a little about what we do at my company, SuccessClinic.com.

At SuccessClinic.com, we help small business owners make more money, help more people, and have more fun. Our mission is to help 10,000 small business owners double their performance and profits.

Yes, it's a big mission...and we're excited about it!

It's true: our mission energizes and focuses us every day. In fact, in the pages that follow, I'll share some remarkable real-life stories from some of my coaching clients who have done exactly that...and even more.

So you're in the right place if you know you're here to make a real difference in the world...

If you want to have a greater IMPACT on people around the world...

And if you want to make more money, help more people, and have more fun.

Because, while you may not believe it, I've got some great news for you...

You have already done most of the heavy lifting necessary to accomplish your big goals and dreams.

I know that might sound far-fetched, even impossible. In fact, you may be thinking...

"What do you mean, I've done most of the heavy

lifting already? I'm nowhere near reaching my big goals, let alone fulfilling my dreams!"

I understand your skepticism, because...

Most of My Clients Were Skeptical, Too

The fact is, most of my clients thought they'd "heard it all before" and that there was nothing new that I could possibly teach them.

Hey, it's understandable, even natural, to have a healthy skepticism. Because most of us have been burned by "gurus" and so-called "experts" who are simply regurgitating old, worn-out ideas that maybe used to work, but don't have any application in our modern world today.

Yet the fact remains that as you read these pages, you might come to understand that some of the things you've been doing up until now just haven't been working for you or serving you.

In fact, you may even come to that "zip lining" moment where life is inviting you to take a step forward...

But your fear and your skepticism will try to hold you back.

Don't worry. Just breathe...

You see, I've helped lots of people through these kinds of problems or "stuck points" from over 75 different industries and more than 120 countries around the world.

So let me repeat what I said a moment ago, but say it

in a different way...

You are closer than you think to achieving your big goals and dreams.

And if you still don't believe me, let me share an embarrassing story with you to show you that...

I Wasn't Always The "Go-To Guy" When It Comes to Making Money

Listen, I want to assure you that I was not always the go-to guy when it comes to getting rid of your head trash around money.

In fact, I was anything but...

December 2006. I had just broken up with my girlfriend and moved back into my parent's house in Maine. Now December in Maine is cold. Freakin' cold.

And I felt as cold inside as the weather felt outside...

At that point in my life, it dawned on me that I was completely broke and it just wasn't going to get any better unless I took ACTION. In fact, I remember that day vividly...

I was sitting in the corner of my parent's basement at this makeshift desk. Really, it was a card table with a folding metal chair. I sat down with a pencil and a yellow legal pad, and added up everything that I owed.

And then it happened...

I discovered that I was $42,000 in credit card debt and I was about to go under. I was beyond depressed. I felt completely worthless.

I felt like I hadn't even lived my life... and yet there was no end in sight, no hope for a better tomorrow.

At That Moment, I Made a Vow

...A promise to God that was like my own personal Declaration of Independence.

I said to myself, "Enough! I will never, ever feel this way again. I'm going to solve this money problem or die trying!"

I swore that I would read every book and go through every course on marketing, success, how to make money...

And I would also pick the brains of the top experts on the planet to discover the real secrets of how to have real financial freedom.

In my journey, I stumbled on a secret formula that gave me financial success, and in this book I'm going to reveal it to you. So just keep reading...

Now remember, even though today I've been very successful helping regular people like you and me to overcome money problems, I'm exactly like you are in so many ways.

I just happened to figure out a really simple, step-by-step formula for the average person like you and me to see massive results when it comes to attracting more abundance and making more money.

The truth is, this step-by-step Formula is designed with YOU in mind.

In fact, it's tailored specifically for people who demand MORE...

More RESULTS... because it empowers you to gain

the recognition and the respect that you deep-down deserve...

Which means you can experience more SECURITY and PROSPERITY...

Enjoy more SELF-CONFIDENCE...

And the ability to OVERCOME ANY OBSTACLE that may be holding you back right now.

And yes, this is the exact Formula that I'll be sharing with you, so you can finally experience RESULTS like these for yourself.

Because you see, the real problem you're facing is not what you think it is...

Are You Struggling?
It's Not All Your Fault

The real reason you're not making the money you desire to be making is not all your fault. Although after you see this, you're going to know that it is your responsibility to take ACTION.

The real problem is the fact that you've been lied to for years.

Yes, it's true: you have been lied to, and these lies are keeping you from the lifestyle and the business you desire and that you deserve.

Let me give you just one example of these lies...

True or false: You have to take huge financial risks in order to make more money and have financial freedom.

That is completely false... but you've probably heard it so many times that you think it's true.

You may have even believed that at one point in your life, but I'm here to tell you that it's not even close to the truth.

The truth is that you can make more money without taking huge financial risks...provided you know and follow the Formula.

Now, if you have believed the lie, I hope you decide to accept the truth now...

Because if you don't, you're going to continue down the road to financial failure and struggle... Your self-confidence is shot...You don't believe in yourself anymore...You don't get to have the impact you want in the world...

And no matter how strong you are, there's a good chance that you'll give up on your dreams, which means you won't be able to take care of your family, you won't make the money or help the people you're here to help...

And ultimately you won't leave the legacy that you really desire to leave on this Earth.

That isn't what I want for you...

And I know it's not what you want for yourself.

So let me repeat...

You CAN make great money without taking huge financial risks...if you follow the Formula.

So if you are struggling to make the money and build the business you really desire, I want you to stop blaming yourself. In fact...

If You Want to Blame Something, Blame This

Now if you really want to blame something, rather than blaming yourself, blame "Information Overload."

All of that misinformation out there is enough to confuse anyone. In fact, it confused me for years. Yet here's the truth you're not going to hear from any of those "gurus"...

You've heard the phrase, "Knowledge is power"?

Well, that used to be true before the Internet, when

knowledge was held by a few powerful, wealthy people.

Now, however, with the popularity of the Internet, each of us has access to a nearly infinite amount of information. Yet with that great access to information, comes another problem...

Because even with all this access to information, there is very little implementation. And information without implementation leads to just one thing...

OVERWHELM.

Which means you stay stuck...

Which means you never finish that project that's on your desk (or in your head)...

Which means you don't get to have real **financial freedom**...(where you have the money you want)...

Or **time freedom** (where you can do what you want, when you want, with whom you want)...

Or **location freedom** (where you can live and work wherever and whenever you choose)...

And that means you don't get to make the money or have the impact...

Or leave the legacy you desire for yourself and the world.

Here's The Truth

The truth is, it breaks my heart to see smart, hard-working entrepreneurs who really want to help people and make a difference, believe it's their fault that they're not making the money and enjoying the success they deserve.

And the net result is that many of these good-hearted people end up giving up on their dreams...

So if you're working hard every day, yet feel like the life is being sucked out of you – well believe me, I know that feeling all too well.

The truth is, I could never go back to that way of living... because it wasn't living at all, merely surviving.

Yet the sad truth is that many people are beating themselves up, giving up on their dreams... which is one of the main reasons I do what I do – to empower hard-working, impact-driven people like you to make more money, help more people, and have more fun.

Okay, now that you know the source of the problem...

And now that you know the truth – that your goal of financial freedom has been held back for years due to these lies...

Let's dive into the 3 massive money mistakes even smart people make that keep them stuck and working way too hard to succeed...

The #1 Massive Money Mistake You Must Avoid If You Want More Success

When I started SuccessClinic.com in my college dorm room in 1997, I had $823 in the bank and a book on how to do html.

The truth is that I had no money, no contacts, no business experience, no sales or marketing training, and no clue how to run a successful business.

All I had was a dream and a desire to help people.

So I built my first makeshift web site – which in those days had no video and only a few tiny images! – and began offering my self-published book which I had printed at the local print shop. (Remember, this was long before the days of Kindle books and print-on-demand.)

And then the strangest thing happened...

People from around the world started to order my book...

Even from countries I'd never heard of...

And people started sending me their stories of how my methods changed their lives and turned their businesses around.

As I would read their stories, I came to realize that there are 3 massive mistakes even smart people make when it comes to making more money.

And if you are doing even ONE of these mistakes, it will severely limit the amount of money you'll make and the amount of people you can help.

That's why it's so important to understand each of these money mistakes, so you can begin to clear them out and make the money and have the impact you truly desire.

The first massive money mistake is *Not getting rid of your head trash around money.*

Here's What It Means

What is your head trash around money?

It's that negative self-talk that tells you, *"I can't do it because..."*

And then you fill in the blank...

- I can't do it because I'm too old...
- I can't do it because I've made too many mistakes...
- Because I didn't graduate from college...
- Because my parents didn't have any money...
- Because I don't live in the right neighborhood...
- Because I can't afford it...

And you know what?

You always make yourself right.

If you believe you can't do it because you're too old, you'll find ways that prove you're too old.

If you tell yourself you can't do it because you can't afford it, you'll never be able to afford it.

If you believe you can't do it because you've made too many mistakes, you'll keep beating yourself up forever.

Here's Why This Is So Important

When you don't get rid of your head trash around money, you're going to experience symptoms like...

- Always chasing the next fad, gimmick, or "marketing trick of the month"...
- Waiting for everything to be "perfect" before taking ACTION...
- Not finishing what you start...
- Not experiencing the income, influence or impact you desire

Now there are basically four vehicles most people use to build wealth. They are...

1. Your retirement account
2. Real estate
3. Investments (stocks, bonds, precious metals, etc.)
4. Your own business

But if you don't get rid of your head trash around money, it doesn't matter which vehicle you use...

Because you'll be driving down the road of life with one foot on the brake.

When You Eliminate This Money Mistake

I want you to picture yourself...

✓ Not having to worry about keeping up with the latest "fad" or "marketing gimmick"...

✓ Not feeling overwhelmed, stressed out, like you're always falling behind...

✓ Having the confidence and self-belief you need to succeed

✓ Recapturing that belief in yourself and your ability to get results

All of this and more is possible, when you get rid of your head trash around money. Isn't that amazing? All of these benefits, just from this one simple tip.

Here's Where to Start

1. Write down three negative beliefs you have about money.

Now you may have more than three negative beliefs about money (in fact, I've identified more than 75 negative beliefs about money that my clients have shared with me). But start with just your top three.

List how those beliefs are affecting your ability to attract more money today.

For example, if you believe, "I can't afford it"...

2. List all the ways that belief is holding you back from making more money.

3. Decide that you're going to rid of your head trash around money.

After doing this exercise, you may find that your head trash around money is costing you a lot more than you think.

That's one reason that simply deciding, today, right now, that you are going to get rid of your head trash around money, will be one of the most important things you can do for yourself, your loved ones, and your legacy.

"I Went from Startup to 7-Figures"

For example, Elizabeth Purvis, an entrepreneur from Portland, Oregon writes...

"When I first came across Noah's work, I'd just started my business and I was confronted with all the 'head trash' that comes along with being a new entrepreneur: uncertainty, who-am-I-to-do-this and a TON of fear. I was barely keeping my head above water – emotionally and financially too. Noah's work came along at a pivotal moment in my life. Today, my company is approaching its first million-dollar year. I will always be grateful to Noah for shining his light and putting his work into the world – it reached me at just the right time!"

I'm sure most of us can relate to having some head trash when we're starting something new – inner beliefs that tell us things like...
"I can't do it"
"This will never work"
"Sure, it worked for others but it won't work for me"
Are you starting to see how having this kind of head

trash around money will keep you stuck and broke? And how getting rid of your head trash around money can set you free?

Here's another example from one of my clients...

"I Went from $60,000 in Debt to 6-Figure Income"

Susan Sherayko from California writes:

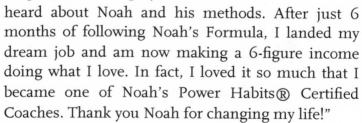

"Before working with Noah, I had spent more than $60,000 on self-help programs and was about to lose everything – my home, my marriage, and was on the verge of bankruptcy. Then I heard about Noah and his methods. After just 6 months of following Noah's Formula, I landed my dream job and am now making a 6-figure income doing what I love. In fact, I loved it so much that I became one of Noah's Power Habits® Certified Coaches. Thank you Noah for changing my life!"

Imagine being $60,000.00 in credit card debt, on the verge of bankruptcy, about to lose your home and your marriage...

And building a 6-figure income in less than a year!

What's even more amazing about Susan's story is that she had spent all that money not on shoes, clothes or frivolous things, but on "gurus" and "self-help" programs.

Yet, not only did those programs NOT help her, they almost wiped her out. It was only after taking that step of faith and following my Formula that her life turned around. Pretty amazing, huh?

Now, how would you like to actually ENJOY the process of making more money?

Well, when you follow my next tip, you can...

The 2nd Massive Money Mistake Even Smart People Make

Imagine that you are enjoying your favorite fun activity with your family and friends...

Maybe you're relaxing on the beach on an island paradise, playing golf or tennis or other fun activity...or maybe you're just enjoying being out in nature, breathing the fresh air of the beach or mountains.

All of a sudden, your phone beeps. You look: What's this? *Hey, it's another order!*

Someone just ordered one of your online programs...

And get this: It happened *without you lifting a finger!*

Your friends look at you and say, "How on Earth can you be making money while you're here with us not working? You used to work all the time and we never even got to see you. What's up??"

Here's what's up: You've eliminated the second massive money mistake that keeps people stuck and working way too hard to grow their business...

Because the second massive money mistake is: *Not having a mentor and trying to do it all by yourself.*

Here's What It Means

A mentor is two things: First, a mentor is someone who's been where you want to go.

For example, maybe you want to increase your income, impact, and influence. Or make more money. Or reach more people with your message.

Well, a mentor is someone who's at the level you want to be at – whether in income, influence, impact – or all three.

However, there is a second, even more crucial aspect to finding the right mentor...

Because a real mentor is someone who can show you the steps of exactly how to go from where you are to where you want to be.

You see, there are plenty of successful people out there. There are lots of people who've made lots of money. And that's great for them...

But have you ever noticed that many of those people who've made a lot of money for themselves won't actually tell you how they did it?

Instead, they send you email after email with bullet-pointed lists about their accomplishments, their awards, their trophies, their wins...

Yet when you look closely, you find that there are shockingly few examples of other people they've helped to succeed.

Here's Why This Is So Important

The right mentor can show you things like how to...
- ✓ Stop trading "time for money"
- ✓ Take ACTION even in the face of fear
- ✓ Trade excuses for RESULTS
- ✓ Get more RECOGNITION and financial rewards
- ✓ Make an IMPACT and enjoy transforming lives around the world

Now I know that might sound like a total dream...

Yet it's a dream that really CAN come true for you, if you follow this simple tip and stop trying to do everything yourself.

Here's Where to Start

1. Write 3 things you want to accomplish in the next 12 months.

For instance, do you want to make more money, increase your influence, take more time off, write a book, launch your online business...? All of the above?

2. Decide who can help you get there.

After you've identified your top 3 goals for the next 12 months, make a list of the people you know or have heard of, who've accomplished similar results, AND... (this is the crucial part)

... Who have helped OTHER PEOPLE get results, too.

In other words, you're looking for a mentor who can give you step-by-step guidance and personal support for YOUR dreams and goals, not someone who just talks about themselves and their accomplishments all day long.

3. Get that person's support to help you achieve your goals.

For example...

"I Made $95,000 in Sales in Just 12 Days"

Brian Lucier, a real estate investor from Massachusetts, writes:

"When I first heard Noah speak at a real estate conference, I was working day-to-day with no clear path or vision. Following Noah's Formula, what used to take hours now takes just 15 minutes. I did $95,000 in sales in just 12 days. Not only that, but I also raised $1.2 million for my church. Thank you Noah – keep doing the work you're doing changing millions of lives!"

Imagine having hours back in your day. What could you do with all that extra time?

Imagine having all that extra energy – because you're

no longer wasting time with things that don't produce RESULTS.

That's why doing this one simple tip can literally change your life.

Here's another example from one of our students...

"I Doubled My Income in 12 Months"

Aubrey Ryan, a business owner from Missouri, writes:

"Before working with Noah, I was working 80 hours a week, never taking a vacation, yet had 15 years of flat sales with no growth. Following Noah's Formula, I doubled my income in 12 months working less than I ever had before!"

Have you heard the phrase "working yourself to death"?

Well, the story behind the story is that when Aubrey first came to me, she had been in a wheelchair because she was literally working herself to death. She had been working 80+ hour work weeks for the previous 15 years. Yet instead of seeing her business grow, her business was stagnant.

In fact, her doctors even told her that she might never walk again. It was that serious.

Yet today she is making MORE and working LESS...

Simply because she followed my Formula.

Now let me share with you the third massive money mistake even smart people make that keeps them stuck.

And let me warn you – this mistake is so crucial, that if you don't follow this next tip, you'll probably keep driving down the road of life with one foot on the brake, which is going to cost you a lot of time, money, and opportunity over the course of your lifetime...

The Crucial Money Mistake You Must Avoid If You Want Financial Freedom

What would it be like if you no longer felt overwhelmed, over-stressed, and overworked?

Suppose there was some way you could stop beating yourself up...

Stop feeling stuck...

And stop feeling like you're always falling behind, working harder and harder just to keep your head above water?

Well, if you stop making this 3rd money mistake, that's what it can feel like for you, too...

Because the third massive money mistake is: *Gathering too much "information" without giving yourself Permission to Succeed®.*

Here's What It Means

You are walking along the beach, enjoying the cool breeze on your face.

You feel the sun kissing your face, hear the relaxing

sound of the ocean waves as they lap upon the beach, and feel the soft sand beneath your feet.

You're with someone you love, and you feel so happy, like you don't have a care in the world.

Then something happens that's totally unexpected...

All of a sudden, you hear someone screaming, "Help! Help!"

You look around – where's that voice coming from?

Suddenly, you look in the ocean and there's someone out there, drowning.

You see them struggling in the water, gasping for air...

What would you do in that moment?

You would do something to help them, right?

If you're a good swimmer, you might immediately jump in the water to save them. Or you might run to get help from a nearby lifeguard. Something, anything to help this drowning person.

So let me ask you a question...

If you saw someone drowning, would you throw them a glass of water?

That would be ridiculous, right?

Yet that's exactly what most people are doing to themselves.

Because we are drowning in information...yet we keep gathering more information without taking ACTION.

On our campus at SuccessClinic.com, we have a saying...

"There is no lack of INFORMATION, but there is definitely a lack of IMPLEMENTATION."

The fact is, most people are drowning in what I call SHELF-HELP.

Shelf-help is that information you keep consuming – from blogs, articles, videos, YouTube, Facebook, Twitter, etc. – without taking ACTION. It's information that sits on the shelf along with all that other information you keep gathering.

Now of course, information can be incredibly useful, especially when it provides insight and shows you how you can save time, money, and/or energy.

However, information only becomes valuable when you combine it with step-by-step guidance, personal mentorship, ongoing support and real-life implementation.

Here's Why This Is So Important

Imagine that you're hungry. It's been a while since your last meal. You feel your stomach growling. You hear your insides gurgling. So you decide to stop what you're doing and get something to eat.

Well, if you keep gathering more "information" without implementation...

It's like knowing 50 ways to get to the grocery store...

And starving to death.

The fact is, if you keep gathering too much

"information" without giving yourself Permission to Succeed®...

You are unconsciously stopping yourself from reaching your goals.

That means you never get to enjoy the things you want to do...

You don't get to have the financial freedom, time freedom, or location freedom you want...

Which means you have to keep working day after day, month after month, year after year without ever getting ahead...

Which means you're not having the impact you want or enjoy the transformation you desire for yourself and the world...

And that leads to more stress, more overwhelm, more frustration...

And that means you're not really living the life you desire – you're just surviving.

That's not what I want for you...

And I know it's not what you want for yourself and your loved ones.

Picture This

Just imagine...

✓ Not holding yourself back from making more money
✓ Getting your foot off the brake in your life, love and career
✓ Not working yourself to the bone, sacrificing family and friends
✓ Not stopping yourself from reaching your

personal and financial goals
✓ Not beating yourself up any more
✓ Feeling that sense of inner peace and self-confidence that highly successful people have
✓ Having more impact, influence, and income
✓ Living the life you dream of

For example...

"I Doubled My Income, Then Doubled It Again"

Mike Camoin from New York writes:
"Before working with Noah, I had spent over $35,000.00 on different programs, but I was still stuck. Following Noah's Formula, I doubled my income in 90 days – then doubled it AGAIN the next 90 days!"

Yes, that's a truly amazing real-life success story from one of my clients. Now let me give you the story behind the story...

You see, I created a program called Power Habits® Academy where I work with a select group of entrepreneurs and personally teach them the Power Habits® of Unconsciously Successful People.

Well, Mike enrolled in my program (which at that time was called the Elite Program), did the exercises I gave him, followed my instructions to the letter...

And doubled his income in just 90 days.

Naturally, Mike was very excited by that result!

Then he heard about my live events, which at that time cost $5,000 per person. Well, he paid the $5,000 and came to our live event, got more personal coaching from me...

Then went back home, followed my instructions again...

And doubled his income AGAIN in the next 90 days.

Just imagine what doubling your income and doubling it AGAIN would do for your family, your lifestyle, your legacy. What kind of things would you do for your family, your friends, your loved ones?

Would you travel more... take more time off... take more vacations... give more to your favorite causes...

Now of course I'm not making any income claims here, because I don't know your specific situation and I don't know how motivated you are to succeed.

However, what I know for sure is that for my coaching clients and students like Mike, Brian, Elizabeth, Susan, Sheila, George, Britnie, Tim, and the thousands of other men and women who have followed my Formula...

The results speak for themselves.

And now it's YOUR turn...

Let's Review Exactly What You Want

Before I share with you my 5-step Formula to get rid of your head trash around money, let me ask you a question...

What is the lifestyle you want to lead and what is the legacy you want to leave for the world?

Lifestyle and Legacy. That's what this Formula is all about.

What do you want in your health?

What do you want in your finances?

What about your spiritual life?

How about your career? Do you want to publish your book? Speak on stages around the world?

What do you want in your relationships?

Whatever your goals are for your lifestyle and legacy, write them down and get very, very clear on what they are.

The Hidden Connection Between Habits and Money

Now you may be thinking, "Okay Noah, this all sounds fantastic. But how does all this work together? Because I want to make more money, help more people, and have more fun. What's the hidden connection between habits and money?"

What I'm about to show you is the one of the main reasons that my clients and I have added over $100 million in sales over the last few years...

Because once you understand the hidden connection between habits and money, everything will start to fall into place for you.

There are two things that create your life. The first thing is the quality of your communication with the world *inside* of you. And the second thing is the quality of your communication with the world *outside* of you.

Your communication with the world inside of you is what I call your Inner Game. Now the Inner Game deals with the things you can't see directly, but that you see the RESULTS of.

For example, you can't see your beliefs, values, desires, thoughts, or decisions. Those things you can't see directly, but you see the EFFECTS of them.

Your communication with the world outside of you is what I call your Outer Game. Those are the things you CAN see directly and that definitely affect your life.

For example, your Outer Game consists of things like your habits, lifestyle, actions, behaviors, systems, and strategies. These are the things you can see directly; the everyday "blocking and tackling" you have to do every day in business. But these are also the things you have to do every day to be successful in your health, your wealth, your family life, your relationships, and so on.

However, it is only when those two things come together, your Inner Game and your Outer Game – only when you master both – do you have the thing called

Success.

Beliefs	S	Habits
Values	U	Lifestyle
Desires	C	Actions
Thoughts	C	Behaviors
Priorities	E	Systems
Decisions	S	Strategies
	S	

Ignore Either One and You're In Trouble

Imagine if you only work on your Inner Game and ignore your Outer Game. That's what I call the "evolved broke person." You're evolved because you've done a lot of spiritual studies and self-help work. But you're broke.

I know this phenomenon very well, because I was that "evolved broke person" – because no one had shown me how to monetize my content. Honestly, I didn't even know what the word monetize meant!

Meanwhile, there are some people who only work on their Outer Game, and ignore their Inner Game. That's where you have the person who has the outer trappings of success – fame, fortune, status, possessions – but somehow, they tend to lose it all.

Why? Because they haven't built the foundation for long-term success. For example, Elvis Presley. River

Phoenix. Andy Gibb. Chris Farley. John Belushi. Lindsay Lohan. Tiger Woods.

The fact is, the pages of history (and on the Internet today) are littered with people who had the appearance of success, but who ended up losing it -- because they didn't have a solid foundation in their Inner Game.

Imagine if you had a house with no electricity. That house is not much fun to live in, because you can't do most of the things we take for granted every day (like watch TV, use the Internet, microwave your breakfast, etc.).

But guess what? While you can't see electricity, you definitely see the effects of it. That's what your Inner Game is like.

Meanwhile, without your Outer Game, you don't have a house in the first place! You're living on a park bench somewhere. That would suck too.

See why we have to master both our Inner Game and Outer Game in order to have the thing called Success?

My $500 Million Proof

This may be counterintuitive, but as I shared with you previously, my clients and I have grown our businesses by more than **half a BILLION dollars** as a result of my teachings.

However, want to hear something incredible? Eighty percent of the cause of that multi-million dollar growth occurred because of work in the Inner Game.

Based on my experience in working with thousands of

clients and students over the last two decades, eighty percent of your success comes from your Inner Game, and only twenty percent comes from your Outer Game.

Now that might not be what you expect – and you may not even believe it right now. That's because it's precisely the opposite of what all those "gurus" are teaching out there.

You've probably taken lots of courses on marketing, sales, and how to grow your business. And of course, that's important. As I mentioned, you can't have success in business without that kind of training.

However, that's all Outer Game.

Yet when you combine Outer Game mastery with Inner Game mastery, your success will not only come much faster, it will last much longer and be far more satisfying, too.

The fact is, most of the people who come to me had spent thousands – even tens of thousands – of dollars on Outer Game training, but had not mastered their Inner Game – only because no one had given them the Formula.

They said to me, "Noah, I've spent all of this money on all these other courses" and were wondering why they hadn't succeeded. The reason was because they hadn't mastered their Inner Game...because no one had shown them how to do it!

Now you may not even realize that there is a Formula to master your Inner Game. But that's exactly what my Formula does – it allows you to master your Inner Game of Success...

Which means you'll stop stopping yourself from success...

And that means you're going to allow yourself to succeed at higher levels than ever before.

I hope that makes you as excited to learn my Formula as I am to teach it to you!

Building Your DREAM Home

Building your business is a lot like building a house. There are a lot of moving parts, a lot of things that go into it. However, because so much of it happens behind the scenes, you don't see it. In fact, the only time you do see it is if it's missing.

Now if you want to build a house, there are basically two ways to do it. The first way is you get up in the morning and say, "Hey, I think I want to build a house!" And you start slapping boards together. And you say to yourself, "I know if I work really hard, a house is going to show up!"

What's wrong with this method? Exactly! There's no plan, no blueprint, no system, no framework...and you're doing it all by yourself. That's why so many people who come to me for coaching or mentoring have a "house" (business) that's pretty drafty... and isn't making them the money they desire.

Can you relate?

Why You Need a Blueprint

The second way to build a house is to start with a blueprint. Maybe you even hire an architect – someone who's done it before, who says, "Sure, I can create blueprints for your dream home."

Now assuming you do choose to go the second way, the first question the architect is going to ask you is... *"What kind of house do you want?"*

How many bedrooms do you want? Do you want 2-car garage or a 3-car garage? What do your want in your kitchen? Do you want tile or marble? How big do you want the living room? And so on.

The point is, there are a lot of decisions that go into building your house. Yet the reality is that it's YOUR house. It's YOUR dream. No one else's.

YOU are the one who's going to live there. That's why it had better be the house that YOU really want.

Then, after you've got the blueprint, you've got your plan, so you simply follow the plan step-by-step every day. When you wake up, you go, "Okay, what do we do today? Here's the checklist, let's get this done!" Because it's right there in front of you, every step of the way.

This way sure is a lot easier and a lot less stressful than slapping boards together!

Stop Struggling Now

Most of the people who come to me have been working really hard, just like I was. Struggling, spending lots of money, working really hard... but they still don't have their dream home.

That's where this Formula comes into play. Why? Because it's a blueprint. A framework. It's a step-by-step, fill-in-the-blank series of checklists.

No more guessing

No more fear.

No more lack.

No more wondering, "What am I supposed to be doing today?"

It's all in the Formula.

Keep reading to see why...

The Income-Happiness Scale

I've got one more thing to show you before we get to the Formula. This is what I call the Income-Happiness Scale.

When I've shared this with my high-level coaching clients, it's been a major "Aha" Experience for them. I even had one woman tell me at one of my seminars that she was going to have the image I'm about to show you tattooed on her shoulder!

While you may not want to go that far, I hope what I'm about to show you will make a difference for you, too.

Now one of the first questions I ask my coaching clients is, *"Why are you in business?"* And I get many answers to that question...

I want to take care of my family.

I want to make a lot of money.

I want to change the world.

I want to make a difference.

I hate working for someone else.

I have a dream to own my own company.

These are just a few of the most common answers. However, when you boil it down, the essential answer to the question of why you are in business is...

You want more INCOME and you want more HAPPINESS.

Now it seems natural and logical that if you want more income and more happiness, that you should focus on those things. Right?

So that's what everyone does – they focus on making money and they focus on trying to be happier. And while there's nothing exactly wrong with that, and that's what everyone focuses on, the fact is that it doesn't work.

Why doesn't it work? Because both money and happiness are the RESULTS of other things.

So rather than focus on money and happiness (the results or outcomes), the truth is that we need to focus on **what causes income** and **what causes happiness.**

What Causes Income and Happiness

So now let me introduce you to the Income-Happiness Scale...

As you can see by the graphic below, we have Income going up the vertical axis and Happiness going across the horizontal axis. The more money you make, the more you go up the vertical axis, and the happier you are, the more you go across the horizontal.

Now the two things that cause Income and Happiness are Activities and Aptitude. *Activities* are the things that you do every day, what you do with the minutes and hours of your day.

Further, there are two kinds of Activities you can do each day – Low-Value Activities and High-Value

Activities.

Aptitude means two things: How good you are at doing each Activity, and how much you enjoy doing it. And there are two aspects of Aptitude: things you Suck At and things you're Great At.

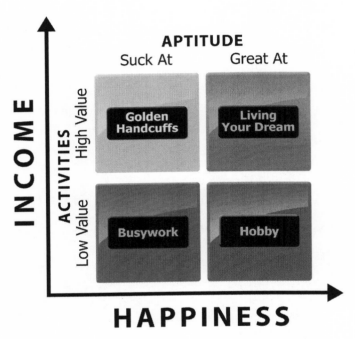

The Hobby Quadrant

Let's start in the lower right-hand corner of the Income-Happiness Scale.

When you have Low-Value Activities that you're Great At (and you enjoy), you have a Hobby. Now there's nothing wrong with having a hobby. All of us should take the time to enjoy hobbies – for example, golf, tennis, gardening, sewing, reading, kayaking, ballroom dancing, and so on.

However, a hobby is not a business. So the question I have for you is: *Do you own a business, or do you own a hobby?*

How can you tell the difference? Simple. With a hobby, you're having fun (see how it's high on the Happiness axis) but you're not making much or any money (see how it's low on the Income axis).

So ask yourself that question, "Do I own a business, or do I own a hobby?"

The Busywork Quadrant

Next, we have Low-Value Activities that you Suck At (and you don't enjoy). That's what I call Busywork.

We live in a world of infinite distractions. You can watch cat videos on YouTube until the end of time. You can waste countless hours on social media. Or you can simply spend hours doing activities that don't grow your business and don't give you either the Income or the Happiness you want.

Notice that in the Busywork quadrant, your Activities aren't producing much money, and you're not enjoying them either. So you don't even get the benefit of having a Hobby. In fact, I once had a client tell me on a coaching call, "Noah, I own a Busywork!"

Do you *own a busywork?* Or are you just spending too much of your valuable time there?

Remember that time is the one resource that can't be replaced!

The Golden Handcuffs

Next we have High-Value Activities that you Suck At. That's what I call the Golden Handcuffs. Let me tell you story to illustrate this quadrant...

At one of our 3-day live events, we had a couple attend from Canada, Dr. Stacey, a chiropractor, and her husband Dean. Dr. Stacey dragged Dean there – literally dragged him.

While he didn't say anything, Dean's body language was very clear: "*Why am I here? I don't want to be here. How can I get out of this?*" (This is a common phenomenon at live events, especially from husbands!)

I could tell just by looking at Dean that he didn't really want to be there. And since this was a 3-day event, I wondered how long he was going to last before he was ducking out the exit.

I took a deep breath and started with my teaching. And then something amazing happened...

In the first 20 minutes, Dean uncrossed his arms. Then he started leaning forward in his chair (a sure sign that someone is interested in what you're saying). Then his jaw dropped open as if he was hearing things that he'd never heard before. Then he started taking notes. Then he started taking A LOT of notes!

By the end of the third day, Dr. Stacey and Dean had signed up for the Inner Circle of my DREAM Mastermind program, where I work with entrepreneurs for one to three years to help them build their dream lifestyle.

Dean told me afterwards that one of the reasons they decided to join my DREAM Mastermind was because he had been in the Golden Handcuffs quadrant for many years. He had been working in a job where he was making 6 figures a year, but he hated his job. He was miserable, unhappy, frequently sick, and so on. But he felt that he couldn't leave that job because he had to take care of his family.

Have you ever been in a situation like that? Where you're making good money but are still unhappy and unfulfilled? That's why I call it the "Golden" Handcuffs – because it's awfully hard to leave a job that pays well, even if you hate it.

Finally, Living Your Dream

And finally, we have High-Value Activities that you're Great At (and that you love to do). That's where you're in the quadrant I call Living Your Dream.

Why is it Living Your Dream? Because when you're doing High-Value Activities that you're Great At AND you love doing, you're not only Living Your Dream – it's like going to heaven without the inconvenience of dying!

When you're Living Your Dream, notice what's happening to your Income. Your Income is going up, but your Happiness is going up, too. In fact, *there is no limit* to the amount of Income you can create, and *no limit* to the amount of Happiness you can experience when you are Living Your Dream. Pretty cool, huh?

The fact is, you CAN Live Your Dream. I know, because I've seen it happen in my own life and in the lives of my clients again and again, when they follow the Formula.

In fact, that's exactly what happened to Dean. He decided to leave the job he hated and start his own landscaping company. Now he's making great money doing what he loves to do, plus he gets to spend time outdoors (which he loves), and he also gets to spend more time with his family, which gives him a great deal of happiness and fulfillment.

Yes, it's truly possible for you, too!

This is one of the wonderful benefits of following the Formula, because you're going to get to the place of Living Your Dream – making more money, helping more people, and having a lot more fun.

It's true: when you're helping people and getting paid to share your message, life becomes amazingly rich, fulfilling and fun.

Now that I've shown you what's possible from following my Formula, let me give you my proven 5-step Formula to get rid of your head trash around money...

Step 1: Get Your Foot Off the Brake Without Using Willpower

Do you ever procrastinate? Do you ever put off doing things you know you should be doing?

When I ask this question in my live events, 80% of the hands go up...and the rest are waiting until later!

Now I think we would all agree that procrastination is not a good thing to do. I'm sure any sane person would agree that procrastination will not only NOT bring you closer to your goals, it will in fact prevent you from reaching your goals in the first place.

Well, if we all agree that procrastination is not a good thing to do, the question is: WHY do we do it? What makes us procrastinate?

Why do we do things that we know won't make us happier, healthier, or wealthier -- when we know we should be doing something different?

The question behind the question, then, is this...

What Is A Habit?

Based on over 20 years of research and working with tens of thousands of clients around the world, I've discovered that there is a simple answer to the question:

"What is a habit?"

In fact, the latest studies from the field of neuroscience reveal that the human brain has developed something called The Habit Loop.

First, The Trigger

The first element of the Habit Loop is called the Trigger. This is *the thing that happens in your world*. You could also call it the *stimulus*.

For example, let's go back to the question of procrastination and why we humans procrastinate. In this example, let's say that you're sitting at your desk, and all of a sudden you think about doing that "thing" that would help you grow your business and make more money.

For instance, you think to yourself, "You know, I really should write that article...or create that blog post... or record that video... or craft that sales letter...or finish that training I started..."

So you are thinking about that activity or action that would actually help you make more money. Let's call that the Trigger in this example.

Next, The Routine

Then we come to the next element of the Habit Loop, called the Routine. That's *the thing you do after the Trigger occurs*.

In this example, you are thinking about doing that activity that will help you make more money. That's the

Trigger.

What is the very next thing you do after the Trigger occurs?

Here's where it gets interesting...

Your brain is highly efficient. We're talking stunningly efficient. That's the good news. However, it's also the bad news.

How could this be both good news AND bad news? Well, because your brain is so highly efficient, when it finds a way of doing things, it doesn't want to change.

Which means that when you start doing something, your brain tends to want to keep doing it, even if you – the owner of said brain – WANT to do something different.

So going back to our procrastination example, you consciously know that procrastinating is not good and that doing this habit is, in fact, costing you time and money.

However, because your brain is so efficient – and it is designed this way in order to keep you alive – your brain essentially says, "Hey, I've got a good thing going here. Why change?"

So you have the *Trigger* (you think about doing that thing that will make you more money)...

And then you do...

Something else!

What's the "something else"?

Well, it could be anything! Watching cat videos on YouTube... checking Facebook... turning on Netflix... going to the kitchen to grab a snack...

The fact is, the distractions – er, possibilities – are endless.

So that becomes your Routine.

Then, The Reward

The third element of the Habit Loop is the Reward. After you do the Routine, the brain releases "happy hormones" called endorphins. These endorphins interact with the receptors in your brain that reduce your perception of pain. Endorphins also trigger a positive feeling in the body, similar to that of morphine.

It's like your brain is saying, "*Ahh! Thanks, I needed that.*"

Think about that for a moment. When you are doing something you enjoy – something you are used to – you actually *feel better.*

But guess what – that is the very problem!

Because you have the Trigger (thinking of doing something that will grow your business), then you do the Routine (doing "something else" that is "easier"), what happens next is the Reward (your brain releases endorphins).

What's going to happen over time? It's pretty obvious, right?

You're going to keep doing that thing that makes you feel good... and keep NOT do that thing that might cause you pain because it's not "easy".

But guess what? *Your brain doesn't care!*

Because your brain gives a Reward (endorphins) for doing things that feel comfortable, your brain doesn't want to start doing things that might make it uncomfortable (might cause pain).

Bottom line: When you try to change your habits

using the old method of "willpower", what you're really doing is trying to fight your own brain.

Do you see why that will never work?

Are you ready to see something else amazing... something that will really blow your mind?

Why Traditional Success Programs Failed You

What I just showed you in the preceding chapter is the #1 problem in the personal growth industry.

Why? Because the personal growth industry is essentially a bunch of programs trying to get us to change our behavior.

Now that makes sense, doesn't it? If we want to get something different, we have to do something different, don't we? So that means changing our behavior, right?

But guess what?

We've been told "how to" change our behavior...when your brain is wired to fight that very thing.

This is why "how-to's" are not enough. If how-to's were enough, we'd all be rich, happy, and thin!

For example, everyone knows "how to" lose weight, "how to" make money, "how to" do whatever it is – what I call the "how-to's" of success.

And how do you know these? Because you've already spent tons of money, time, and effort reading all those books, buying all those programs and going to all those seminars!

But, because your brain gets a Reward for doing a habit, it doesn't want to change. That's why you can know "how to" do something... And never actually let yourself do it.

Why "How-to's" Are Not Enough

Because traditional success programs focus almost exclusively on the "how-to's" of success, when you try to use those programs to get unstuck, stop procrastinating, or let yourself succeed...

It's like trying to drive a nail in the wall...*using a chainsaw.*

You have been given the wrong tool.

Now there's nothing "wrong" with a chainsaw. However, if you want to drive a nail into the wall, it's the wrong tool for the job.

And this is why the thousands of clients who have come to me, had spent so much time, money, and effort on all of those "money-making" programs... but were still STUCK.

Why You're Closer Than You Think

But guess what?

You are closer than you think to achieving your goals.

How do I know this? Because you've already done the heavy lifting. You've spent time, money, and effort on all those other programs.

However, what many people have told me after joining my online courses, coming to my live events or having me mentor them is that this is *the last personal growth program they ever needed.*

Now that is a very powerful statement.

From now on, stop trying to use willpower to change your habits...because trying to use willpower to change your habits is like trying to dig a gold mine with a teaspoon.

Here's What to Do Next

1. Write 3 things you want to accomplish in the next 12 months.
2. Go back to that list you made earlier. (You did make that list, right? Or did you, ahem, put it off?)
3. Examine your habits.
4. After you've identified your top 3 goals for the next 12 months, list the habits you're doing that are stopping you or holding you back from reaching those goals.
5. Get clear on how you'll benefit from facing your fears.

For example...

"I Built a 7-Figure Business in Just 2 Years"

Tim Taylor, one of my clients, writes...

"Before working with Noah, I was holding myself back out of fear. As a result of working with Noah, I built a 7-figure

business in less than 2 years. If you get the change to work with Noah, just
do it – because I know it will change your life like it changed mine!"

We have a saying on our SuccessClinic.com campus – we call it "3 years to 7 figures." That's because we see clients time
and again who are able to take my Formula and build their dream lifestyle business in that amount of time.

Now Tim was able to build it in just under 2 years. And that's awesome...

The point here is that before using my Formula, Tim was holding himself back out of fear. He had spent tens of thousands on other programs but was still stuck.

Yet when he started using my Formula, it was like he got shot out of a cannon... because he took what I showed him and literally changed his life.

Now let's go to Step 2...

Step 2: Engage Your Loving Mirrors

Imagine that you are standing at the edge of a cliff and you're looking at where you want to go. So you're standing "here" and you're looking "over there" which is where you want to be.

Here's what it looks like...

Right now, you are in what I call your Current Perceived Reality (CPR). And where you want to get to is what I call your New Desired Reality (NDR).

In your CPR, you do what you do, you have what you have, you know what you know, and you are what you are. That is what you perceive your reality to be.

And your NDR is all the things you WANT – more money, more impact, more influence, a new car, a better job, happier relationships, world peace, and so on.

But between your CPR and your NDR, there is a gap. And that gap is what I call Your Belief Gap.

For example, maybe you want to write a book, get your word out in a bigger way, have more clients, grow your revenues, or whatever it might be. Now if I were to ask you, "Do you think you can do that?" You'd probably say, "Sure I can do it!"

That's your *conscious* mind talking.

But if we could hear what you were telling yourself in your *subconscious* mind, we'd probably hear things like, "I don't know if I can do it. I don't know how I'm going to do it. What if I'm not good enough?"

Why You Need a Loving Mirror

After working with thousands of coaching clients and Mastermind students over the last 20 years, I've come to realize that without someone who believes in you, it's awfully hard to believe in yourself.

How do I know this?

Well, I've had the privilege of interviewing more than 100 millionaires and multi-millionaires, including the biggest names in the industry. And the fact is every one of these highly successful people had someone believe in them BEFORE they believed in themselves.

That is what I call having a Loving Mirror. A Loving Mirror is someone who believes in you before you believe in yourself.

"I Went from $5,000 to $75,000 per Month"

One of our graduates, Sheila Valles from California, writes...

"Before working with Noah, I was working 70 hours a week and making $5000 a month in sales. As a result of working with Noah, our sales grew to over *$75,000 per month.* Thank you Noah for taking the lid off of my thinking and letting me know I can have the BEST!"

Now here's the story behind the story...

Sheila and her husband, David, attended one of my seminars. Prior to that day, they'd never even heard of me. However, at the end of my program, Sheila and David came up to our table where we were taking enrollment into one of my courses.

At that time, the program cost $3,000 so Sheila was going back and forth, basically asking herself, "Should I sign up? Shouldn't I?" A lot of hemming and hawing.

Finally David reached into his wallet, took out his American Express Card, handed it to me and said, "Honey, this is different. You're getting this!"

Sheila later told me that it wasn't that she doubted my

program or the results. Sheila was doubting *herself.*

Because she, like so many others, had spent so much money on all the "how to succeed" programs out there. So she naturally thought, "How can this be any different? I'm sure it's the same old stuff."

But as Sheila and so many others have found out, this actually IS different. For her, it was the missing piece to her success puzzle... and the results speak for themselves.

See a Pattern Here?

Yes, it's true: The pattern is that most of the people come to me after spending a lot of money on all the big-name "gurus" -- yet they were still stuck.

Then these smart, hard-working people hired me, started following my Formula...

And for the first time, started making more money, working less, and enjoying life more than ever before.

By the way, the case studies I'm sharing with you in this book are ordinary people who've gotten extraordinary results, because they took ACTION and followed the Formula.

Here's What to Do Next

1. Look at your goals list from Step 1.
2. Identify 3 people who can support you in reaching your goals.
3. They may be people in your life right now, or they may be people like a mentor or coach who can help you get their faster and easier.
4. Enlist their support to reach your goals.

You may need to go back to Step 1 and get clear how you're going to benefit from facing your fears of asking for help.

Which brings us to Step 3...

Step 3: Install Systems that Make Your Success Automatic

Think for a moment about your house. What is your house, really? At its core, your house consists of two things — Structure and Systems. Your house's *Structure* is its particular style – Cape, Ranch, Victorian, etc. – and includes how its individual parts are arranged: the number of rooms, how big the rooms are, where they're placed, and so on. That's the Structure of your house.

Secondly, your house consists of *Systems*. Systems make the Structure of your house *serve a particular function*. Your house's Systems include: electric, heating, ventilation, plumbing, and so forth. These Systems make your house *a space in which you can live comfortably*. That is the function of a house.

If your house's Systems don't work properly, you've got a building sitting there that's not much fun to live in.

Now when is the only time you ever think about the Systems in your house? Exactly: when they break. The only time you ever think about your plumbing is when your drain gets stopped up. You never think about electricity until you go to turn on a light and nothing happens.

Think about your body. Your body is like a house,

SIMPLIFY   PEOPLE

INCOME

INTROSPECTION   ACTIVITIES

ENVIRONMENT

because your body is also composed of *Structure* and *Systems*. The Structure of your body is your basic makeup: whether you're male or female, tall or short, and your individual features and genetic characteristics.

Then, your body consists of Systems. The function of your body's Systems is for you to *remain alive*. Your body contains dozens of interdependent Systems: circulatory, muscular, skeletal, nervous, respiratory, immune... plumbing!

And when is the only time you ever think about these Systems? You got it: when they break.

You never think about your respiratory system unless you suddenly can't breathe; or think about your digestive system until you're in the doctor's office going, "Gee, maybe I shouldn't have eaten those dozen chocolate donuts..."

If the Systems of your house or your body aren't working at optimal levels, you have a bunch of parts that don't serve the function you want. Well, it's the same with your *life* and your *business*.

Your life and your business also consist of Structure and Systems. But here's where we run into...

What's Missing From Most People's Lives

1. Most people have no idea what the Systems of their lives or businesses are.
2. They don't know how to fix the Systems when they're broken.
3. They keep calling an "electrician" when they have a "plumbing problem"!

Well, you can stop running around now...

Because I've identified the 5 Essential Systems that you need to be operating properly, in order to have a life and a business that perform the functions you want, and give you the freedom you desire.

The 5 Essential Systems of Support™ for your life and your business are your People System, your Activities System, your Environment System, your Introspection System, and your Simplify System.

People, Activities, Environment, Introspection and Simplify. Each one has its own individual set of rules, and requires its own set of habits, to keep them operating at optimal levels.

It doesn't matter if you're married or single, male or female, whether you're an entrepreneur or you work for someone else. The Systems remain the same.

That's why, if you're not making the money you want to be making, one of the first things you should do is examine your Systems.

For example, if you're making $10,000 per month, you have $10,000 per month Systems.

If you're making $100,000 per month, you have $100,000 per month systems.

And if you're making a million dollars a month, you have million-dollar per month systems.

"I Went from 80-Hour Work Weeks to 6-Figure Months"

For example, George Rivera from Austin, Texas writes...

"Before Noah, I was working like a slave 80 hours a week as an employee. Since being mentored by Noah, I now own my own business that brings in six figures per month. Plus, I found the love of my life thanks to following Noah's Formula. Thank you Noah for believing in me when no one else did!"

The point is that once you install these Systems of Support at higher levels, your income and your happiness can't help but go up.

Here's What to Do Next

1. Look at the Systems of Support graphic in this

chapter.

2. Rate yourself on a scale from 1 to 10 in each of the Systems with 1 being "poor" and 10 being "perfect".

3. For example, if you have a great People System, rate yourself 8 or above. But if you need help in that area, rate yourself 5 or lower. Do the same for each of the Systems of Support.

4. Make a plan to improve your rating in each System over the next 90 days.

Now let's go to Step 4...

Step 4: Heal Your Relationship with Money

How many negative thoughts have you had about yourself in your lifetime? A million? A billion? A million billion kajillion?

For most of us, we probably couldn't count that high!

For example, what stories do you tell yourself about money? Because that's one area where many people have a lot of head trash.

Try this simple exercise. Finish these sentences:

Money is…

Rich people are…

Being wealthy is…

The reason I can't have a lot of money is…

Trying to earn a lot of money is…

When we do exercises like this in our live events, many people are shocked to discover their hidden head trash around money.

Whether you realize it or not, you have a relationship with money. However, most people have a relationship with money that's keeping them from getting the very thing they want. That's one reason you must heal your relationship with money if you want to make more money and be a lot happier.

Do You Have A Dysfunctional Relationship with Money?

The fact is, you have a relationship with money, just like you have relationships with the people in your life.

The way that I often describe this to my clients is to think of money as a person. *If you treated a person the way you treat money, would money want to be around you?*

Are you angry at money? Do you demean money or put it down? Are you ashamed or embarrassed to talk about money or be around it? Do you think money is "dirty"? Do you think people who have a lot of money are "bad" or somehow not as "spiritual" as you?

Well, do you think a person whom you treated that way would want to be around you?

Think about it. If you keep telling yourself, "I can't afford it" (whatever "it" is), then what you're really saying to money is, "I don't want you around."

Now I know you might think this sounds awfully woo-woo. However, based on my personal experience and that of my clients and students, if you don't heal your relationship with money, you're going to be run by your head trash around money...

Which means your ability to make and receive money will be severely limited.

80% of Your Success Is Inner Game

Remember what I shared with you earlier – that 80% of your success comes from your Inner Game. That's why I encourage you to examine your relationship with money and, if there's something in that relationship that's dysfunctional or not optimal, to take action to heal your relationship with money.

Please note that if you don't heal your relationship with money, that dysfunctional relationship will show up throughout your life in many ways.

For example, would you like to publish a book? Become a bestselling author? Speak on stages around the world? Increase your income, impact and influence?

Well maybe you've been wanting to do these things for a long time. But instead of, for example, writing your book, you keep saying to yourself, "I'll do it when I have the time" or "I'll do it whenever."

What is 5/8ths of the word *whenever?*

Exactly: NEVER!

My point is this: If you don't heal your relationship with money, you will keep putting off doing things that will, in fact, make you more money.

However, once you do heal your relationship with money, you will eliminate distractions, you'll become focused and energized, and you will attract more money almost automatically.

Here's What to Do Next

1. Do the sentence completion exercise from this chapter.
2. Write your relationship with money on a scale from 1 to 10.
3. With 1 being "poor" and 10 being "perfect".
4. Make a plan to improve your relationship with money over the next 90 days by following these steps.

Now let's go to Step 5...

Step 5: Step Into Your Best Future

In this book, I've talked a lot about your Inner Game and why it's so essential to your success. But there's another phrase that I use on our campus all the time, and it's this...

"One positive ACTION is worth a thousand positive thoughts."

Yes, it's important to think positive.

Yes, it's important to believe in yourself.

Yes, you have to master your Inner Game in order to succeed.

But, if you want to have your "dream home" (your Dream Lifestyle), the fact is that you've got to swing a hammer to make it happen.

You must take ACTION, because your house won't magically build itself.

It Ain't What You Know...

The famous author and humorist Will Rogers had a great quote: "It ain't what a man don't know that gets him in trouble. It's what he knows that ain't so."

Isn't that true?

What if all the limiting beliefs – all the "I can't do its"

– that you've been telling yourself all these years turned out to be lies?

Well, guess what... They ARE lies.

We've all heard them. We all have them.

But you can't listen to them, or it's going to kill your business, crush your dreams, and you will keep holding yourself back from Living Your Dream.

Here's more proof of that...

Back in the early 1990's, when I began my spiritual studies, I started reading books by authors like Louise Hay, Deepak Chopra, Marianne Williamson – all the classics. I was living in Los Angeles at the time, working at big movie studios.

Well I started dreaming of writing books and having my books published by Hay House, because I saw that Hay House was the publisher of many of my favorite authors.

But as I was dreaming that dream, I also heard a voice in my head that said things like, *"Who do you think you are? That'll never happen for you. Who's going to listen to you? Hay House is only for the 'big guys'. It's for someone else, but not me!"*

Dump Your Head Trash and Take Action

Well, you already know the rest of the story...

My surprising result is that I did end up becoming a Hay House author, *in spite of my head trash* that said it would never happen for me.

It's so humbling to be mentioned in the same breath

with the biggest names in the industry. And it's incredible to meet so many amazing people just like you from around the world who've changed their lives using my Formula.

So if you're still hearing that inner voice that says "it'll never happen for you," I'm inviting you to stop listening to that guy.

Just imagine what could happen to you if you stopped listening to that bully in your head and let yourself dream again...

And say to yourself, *"Wait a minute...If he can do it, I can do it too."*

Then you can have a dream with a vision.

A dream with a vision means, *"No matter what it takes, I'm building my dream home. I'm not taking 'no' for an answer. No matter what I have to do, nothing is going to hold me back from Living My Dream."*

However, if you just dream without taking ACTION, then your house won't get built.

Which means your dreams won't come true...

And that means you'll be left dreaming about your dream life instead of Living Your Dream.

By the way, most people end up giving up on their dreams, which means they often end up in the "Golden Handcuffs" that I showed you earlier.

The fact is that Mike, Susan, Sheila, Aubrey, Tim, George, Brian and all of the other people whose stories I've shared with you in this book (and so many others) are ordinary people who got extraordinary results simply by following my Formula.

And now, you can too...

Here's What to Do Next

1. Write 5 limiting beliefs you have about money.
2. List how these limiting beliefs are holding you back from making the money and making the difference you desire.
3. Decide what you're going to do in the next 7 days to take ACTION to Live Your Dream, and stop being defined by your past.

What Now?

Right now, as we near the end of this book, you have 2 simple choices...

Option 1: Take all the tips I've just shared with you and try to put the puzzle pieces together on your own without any help.

Yes, it will take longer and yes, you'll probably make some painful, costly mistakes... but you can do it this way if you choose. In fact, that's what the average person will do, because it seems "easier".

However, there's the smarter choice...

The simple step that successful people take to speed their progress toward success and victory...

Because why go at this alone, when I've done all the work for you?

Why not give yourself the gift of *peace of mind?*

Because not only have I laid out your exact, step-by-step blueprint...

The fact is that you don't have to reinvent the wheel any longer.

Why? Because my methods have been tried and tested by more than 100,000 successful men and women around the world...and proven to work, guaranteed.

Option 2: Do what smart, savvy men and women around the world have decided to do – join...

Money Mindset Mastery
Business Lifestyle Training

This program will give you the fastest, best and most effective way to rapidly increase your income, impact and influence... guaranteed.

Why? Because my radically simple system will work for you, even if you have...

✓ A super-busy schedule (this is lifestyle-friendly)

✓ Tried a bunch of other things in the past

✓ Low self-esteem or your self-confidence has been shot

✓ People in your life who don't believe you can achieve your dreams;

Or...

✓ Even if you THINK you've tried everything already.

If You've Got 20 Minutes a Week, I Guarantee To Work a Financial Miracle In Your Life.

Because in my Money Mindset Mastery course, I give you my proven, research-backed money and mindset methods and strategies that have produced more than **half a BILLION dollars** for me and my clients.

Here's What You'll Get

In-depth training and Q&A Coaching Calls

You'll get customized, in-depth skill-building training calls from a lifestyle and business mentor who's directly responsible for more than half a billion dollars in sales.

And because we limit the number of people who can join this exclusive group, you're guaranteed to get your questions answered, even the hard ones.

Which means you'll get the kind of personal collaboration and step-by-step guidance from a 20-year business-building expert that you can't get with any other program.

Network with other successful business leaders

Want to quickly grow your revenues? The fastest way is to uplevel the quality of your relationships. You'll meet other successful entrepreneurs who can help you skyrocket your career.

Learn in community

You'll also gain access to our private networking group and get honest feedback from fellow business leaders... which means you never have to feel alone again...

And that means you can stop spinning your wheels and start living the life you've imagined.

What Makes This So Different?

When it comes to making more money, many entrepreneurs are drowning in "too much information" – which means you're not taking action or getting the RESULTS you truly desire.

Money Mindset Mastery helps you get out of overwhelm so you can rapidly start making more money without having to work so hard.

We know how hard it is to conquer fear and procrastination and have helped thousands of business owners to get rid of their head trash about money.

And when you get rid of your head trash, your sales instantly **accelerate**...

...Your **revenues** increase practically overnight...

...You feel that sense of **confidence** and belief in yourself that you may have lost...

...Your team members become an **unstoppable force**...

...And that means you're going to be **happier** and a lot more **successful**!

When You Join This Exclusive Club, You Will...

1. **Discover how to make more money, help more people, and have more fun.** You will completely understand how to get out of your own way without having to use willpower or "psych yourself up."

2. **See how this formula has been used** by more than 10,000 successful business owners around the world.

3. **Apply this framework to your life and business.** You will unlock your hidden power to succeed in money, health, relationships, and your family life.

Plus, This Limited-Time Bonus

✓ 12-Month Access to "Abundant Lifestyle Mastermind" ($1,164.00 Value)

This is our private community of success-minded people from around the world... Like-minded men and women who are facing the same struggles you're facing...

Which means this is the perfect opportunity to connect with others who are going through what you're going through every day...

So you can share ideas, even joint venture...

Which means you can stop trying to re-invent the wheel and stop working so hard to get ahead!

Our "No Student Left Behind" Policy

When you work with us at SuccessClinic.com, you're a student... not just a "customer".

That's because – and I know this may sound old-fashioned – but we genuinely CARE about you and your success.

Plus, I'm on a mission to change our industry for the better...

Because I'm tired of all the hucksters and self-proclaimed "gurus" who are great at marketing, but who suck at teaching.

That means that not only will we be working together in this program...

You'll also get our Heroic Customer Support that's become our hallmark.

Which means you'll get your questions answered, you'll never feel alone, and you'll get the "Star Treatment" we've become famous for.

Here's What This Will Do For You

You'll get rid of your head trash around MONEY ...

Which means you'll finally be able to FINISH that project sitting on your desk (or in your head) forever...

Which means you'll be able to ATTRACT a lot more money into your life...

And that means you'll have the CONFIDENCE to do the things you really desire to do...

Which means you'll have more IMPACT and

TRANSFORM lives around the world...
And that means you'll leave a LEGACY of goodness and happiness for your children and the world!

This Is For You If...

✓ You're frustrated by not having the income and happiness you want.

✓ You want personal guidance to get from where you are to where you want to be.

✓ You want to get rid of your head trash and stop holding yourself back

✓ You desire to get more out of every investment you'll make for the rest of your life.

This Is NOT For You If...

✓ You're looking for a "get-rich-quick" scheme where you don't have to do any work.

✓ You don't care about making a difference or having an impact.

✓ You don't like step-by-step personal help.

✓ You like working alone and don't want someone there helping you get real RESULTS.

What's My Investment?

How much is your head trash costing you right now?
How many potential customers are you missing out on because of procrastination and overwhelm?
How many clients went to someone else because you

didn't communicate your value effectively?

How many people are passing up your offers? Can you honestly reach your goals if you keep doing what you're doing?

Bottom line: Not getting rid of your head trash may already be costing you a great deal.

Remember The Zip Line?

Remember that zip line story I told you at the beginning of this book?

When you're presented with an opportunity to make a quantum leap in your life – to do get better results without having to work so hard – you have 3 options...

1. Go back the way you came (ignore the opportunity)
2. Stay right where you are (don't take any action); or
3. Take a step of faith.

Notice that I didn't call it a "leap of faith." That's because in those life-defining moments, just like my zip lining experience, it often isn't a leap... it's simply a step.

For example, when you met that "special someone," you probably didn't have to leap over tall buildings to meet them.

But you probably had to take a step to walk with them for the first time!

Learning how to drive, graduating from school, walking down the aisle – all of these life-changing moments are STEPS, not leaps.

And, just like my zip line story, when you take that first step towards your new, happier, wealthier, healthier, more successful, more prosperous, more abundant life...

My team and I will be right here on the other side to catch you and give you the VIP Treatment you deserve!

One Final Guarantee

While there aren't many guarantees in life, there is one thing I know for sure...

If you choose to do nothing, nothing will change. As you know, the definition of insanity is *doing the same thing and expecting different results*.

Yes, it takes ACTION...

Yes, it takes COMMITMENT...

But if you're not where you want to be in life...

If you want to get unstuck and finally get rid of your head trash around money once and for all...

You owe it to yourself to take this step into your new, more abundant future.

One More Embarrassing Fact You Need to Know About Me

Let me conclude by sharing this rather embarrassing fact about myself with you...

I never intended to be an entrepreneur.

It's true: my first attempts to build my business were dismal failures. I assumed, like you may be doing yourself, that I just didn't have what it takes to succeed – that I didn't have the skills, that it just wasn't meant to be.

I ended up spending over $250,000 on "gurus" and so-called "experts" that couldn't teach their way out of a paper bag. That's why I vowed to create the easiest, most effective, most results-getting programs to help people around the world...

And create a business that wasn't just about making a profit – but more importantly, about transforming lives.

After I finally succeeded, I stumbled on my Formula quite by accident. The truth is, I was just looking for a way to pay my bills and get out from under the sucking crush of credit card debt. Yet when that took off, I made millions.

Today I've been blessed to teach these methods to thousands and thousands of men and women who are making millions and millions of dollars themselves.

And despite my lack of natural talent, I became the most sought-after mentor of how to get rid of your head trash and make more money in the industry.

It's through that experience of so-called "failure" that I learned a very simple lesson that I want to share with you today...

Talent Cannot Out-Perform a Formula

It's true: Talent and hard work alone are NOT enough to create true, lasting success.

However, simply following my Formula that has empowered folks like you from around the world to duplicate, and even surpass, my own financial success.

And now it's your turn...

Here's What To Do Next

Because you're reading this book, join
Money Mindset Mastery at this private web page...

NoahStJohn.com/get-mastery-now

I look forward to being a part of YOUR Success Story!

Who Is Noah St. John?

Noah St. John is a keynote speaker and bestselling author who's famous for inventing Afformations® and helping small business owners make more money, help more people, and have more fun. His sought-after advice is known as the "secret sauce" in business and personal growth.

According to Stephen Covey, author of *The 7 Habits of Highly Effective People*: "Noah St. John's work is about discovering within ourselves what we should have known all along – we are truly powerful beings with unlimited potential."

Noah's dynamic and down-to-earth speaking style always gets high marks from audiences. As the leading authority on how to eliminate limiting beliefs, Noah delivers keynote speeches and mastermind programs that have been called "The only training that FIXES every other training!"

He also appears frequently in the news worldwide, including ABC, NBC, CBS, Fox, The Hallmark Channel, National Public Radio, Chicago Sun-Times, Parade, Los Angeles Business Journal, The Washington Post, Woman's Day, Chicago Sun-Times, Entrepreneur on Fire, Selling Power, Forbes.com, The Jenny McCarthy Show, Costco Connection and The Huffington Post.

Fun fact: Noah once won an all-expenses-paid trip to Hawaii on the game show Concentration, where he missed winning a new car by three seconds. (Note: He had not yet discovered his Afformations® or Power Habits® Systems.)

Book Noah to speak and discover our full range of business and personal growth programs at

Noahstjohn.com

Recommended Resources

Book Noah St. John
For Your Event

Unify your team • Get out of overwhelm • Grow your business

Tired of "motivational" speakers who don't say anything useful?

Book Noah St. John to speak for your group and discover why CEOs, NFL athletes, working moms, and entrepreneurs worldwide call Noah's programs "MANDATORY for anyone who wants to succeed in life and business!"

Noah's Most Requested Topics

✓ **The Peak Performance Edge:** How to Win the Mental Game for Ultimate Success

✓ **The Automatic Sales Formula:** Building Your 24/7 Automated Selling Machine

✓ **The 5 Principles of Hypergrowth:** How to Achieve More in a World of Infinite Distractions

"Definitely NOT your typical motivational speaker! I took 6 pages of notes in the first 30 minutes of Noah speaking. *SIMPLY PHENOMENAL – A MUST-HAVE RESOURCE for every organization!*"

Carol Stoops, Senior National Sales Director, Mary Kay

"Noah St. John is the smartest, most effective teacher and seminar leader/trainer I have ever come across. Noah will not only get your people motivated, he'll send them away with the step-by-step tools to produce results!"

Casandra Hart, Isagenix

"All I heard was great feedback -- Thank you Noah for really engaging the audience! I am recommending you as a speaker for more chapter meetings."

Heather Gortz, Meeting Planners International

"WAHOO! Finally, a COMMON SENSE APPROACH to success."

Charlotte Edwards, U.S. Air Force

Book Noah for your event at

BookNoah.com

Become The Unstoppable Success Machine You Were Born to Be

What will you do when lack of time, energy, relationships, and money are no longer an issue for you? Get Unstuck Now is designed specifically for mission-driven entrepreneurs and agents of change who want to use what you HAVE to get everything you WANT.

✓ Get paid to do what you're great at
✓ Gain more energy than you've had in years
✓ 8 fast and easy ways to remove bottlenecks even if you feel totally stuck right now

Try Get Unstuck Now at
TryGetUnstuckNow.com

Record Your Own Personalized Afformations® Audios

With just a few simple clicks, you'll have your own personalized audio recordings with the Afformations® and music of your choice. Then sit back, listen, and watch your dreams manifest faster and easier than you ever thought possible!

- ✓ You want to quickly and easily create your own customized
- ✓ Afformations Audios you can listen to anytime, anywhere.
- ✓ You're not a "techie" and want an easy, step-by-step way to make your audio recordings.
- ✓ You want to attract more abundance on autopilot

Get Afformware now at

Afformware.com/start

Take a Quantum Leap in Your Life & Business

Yes, you CAN have your Dream Lifestyle... even if you think you've "tried everything." Because in this 12-month high-level immersion program, Noah will personally walk you step-by-step through his proven methods that have made him and his clients MILLIONS. Do you have what it takes to be part of the DREAM Mastermind Family? (Application only)

This is for you if...

✓ You're ready to have a 6- or 7-figure online business that runs on autopilot

✓ You've tried lots of things in the past but still aren't getting the results you want

✓ You want to join a supportive family of mission-driven entrepreneurs to help you live your dreams

Apply now at
TheDreamMastermind.com

Made in the USA
Columbia, SC
30 October 2017